AF291239

The Crystal Heart Bottle Stopper:
The Offense

RIVER

ISBN: 978-1-5356-1778-9

For years my daughter and I would walk the shores of Lake Erie to calm our souls. We would search for beach glass and listen to the calming waves. They seemed to have a way of bringing us back to a point in ourselves where we could face what was happening to us and talk about it. We would walk in silence for hours, hearing only the sounds of the shore around us, until she was ready to talk about the ongoing painful actions that she had to endure from her father. Each time she went to court-ordered visitation we never knew if he would bring her home as scheduled or finally kidnap her for good, for he threatened it almost every time. Sometimes he would just not bring her home or not let her talk to me for weeks, starting from the age of three. I was trapped because her father deceived the judge and convinced him that I did not let her see him (when at that time, he saw her almost every day) and the judge told me if I did not give her father overnight visitation he would take her from me permanently and give her to him. The mind games her father played were unbearable for me and my daughter and sometimes words just could not surface from our souls until we could rest our minds.

One day while we were searching, we found a crystal-heart bottle stopper in the sand. As we continued to walk the shore, my daughter and I started to make up stories about how it might have gotten there. When my daughter started one idea for a scenario, I realized she was cleansing her soul and talking about herself and representing her fears through lovable characters. I ran to the car to get my writing journal and we sat down on the beach, right then, and wrote our story (in rough form) that we are about to share with you. When my daughter and I formally started working on this first book together, we decided to have River and Rain represent us. We carefully decided on their character traits. We wanted them to match ours so our familiar readers would know that they are a part of us in this heart-wrenching story that reflects how our lives have been for the past ten years. We were going through a dreadful time with my daughter's father, and writing this book gave us a way to express our feelings and give validity to our ongoing trauma.

Although we have created some fictional characters for our book, they too are there for specific, valid reasons and they represent relationships in our life. The context was changed slightly to protect my daughter's privacy. I am sharing this book in hopes that when a parent and child read it together, it might ignite conversations and help give the child vocabulary to express their own feelings about difficult and confusing topics. We wanted to put something gentle in the hands of their parent that helps them to create an experience of self-discovery and healing for the child after they have been wounded by another adult caregiver. It is tricky for the abused parent to talk with their child in a way that includes the truth but does not damage the child any further by criticizing the other parent and bringing the child into more adult conflict. The important thing to happen is for the child to express how they feel and what they believe about themselves and the adults around them. How do they see their world after the trauma has left their lives in shambles? As they look through the wreckage, trying to salvage something familiar and safe, they are trying to find who they are and to figure out if their world still makes sense.

Looking for beach glass and finding the crystal-heart bottle stopper is a metaphor for us looking for answers and finding them in ourselves. Writing this book was a turning point and it initiated our journey back to each other. This book is setting the stage, so to speak, for the following books, when we will begin to dig deeper into our souls and learn how to gather inner strength and let healing begin.

Going through a divorce because of abuse is one example of a trauma that a child might experience. If one parent is abusive or controlling, the parent and child who are the victims are left in pieces. No matter how much the mother loves her child, she is taking care of her own wounds and the child can be left tending to their own despair at times. Words get left unsaid. Rain and River feel each other's pain and find their way back to each other in this book. In the following books, they find themselves on a journey of facing and attaining healing of past trauma, plus bonding again and moving on together. Their strength is being built during the process of enduring the heartache and making it through to the other side where their healing awaits.

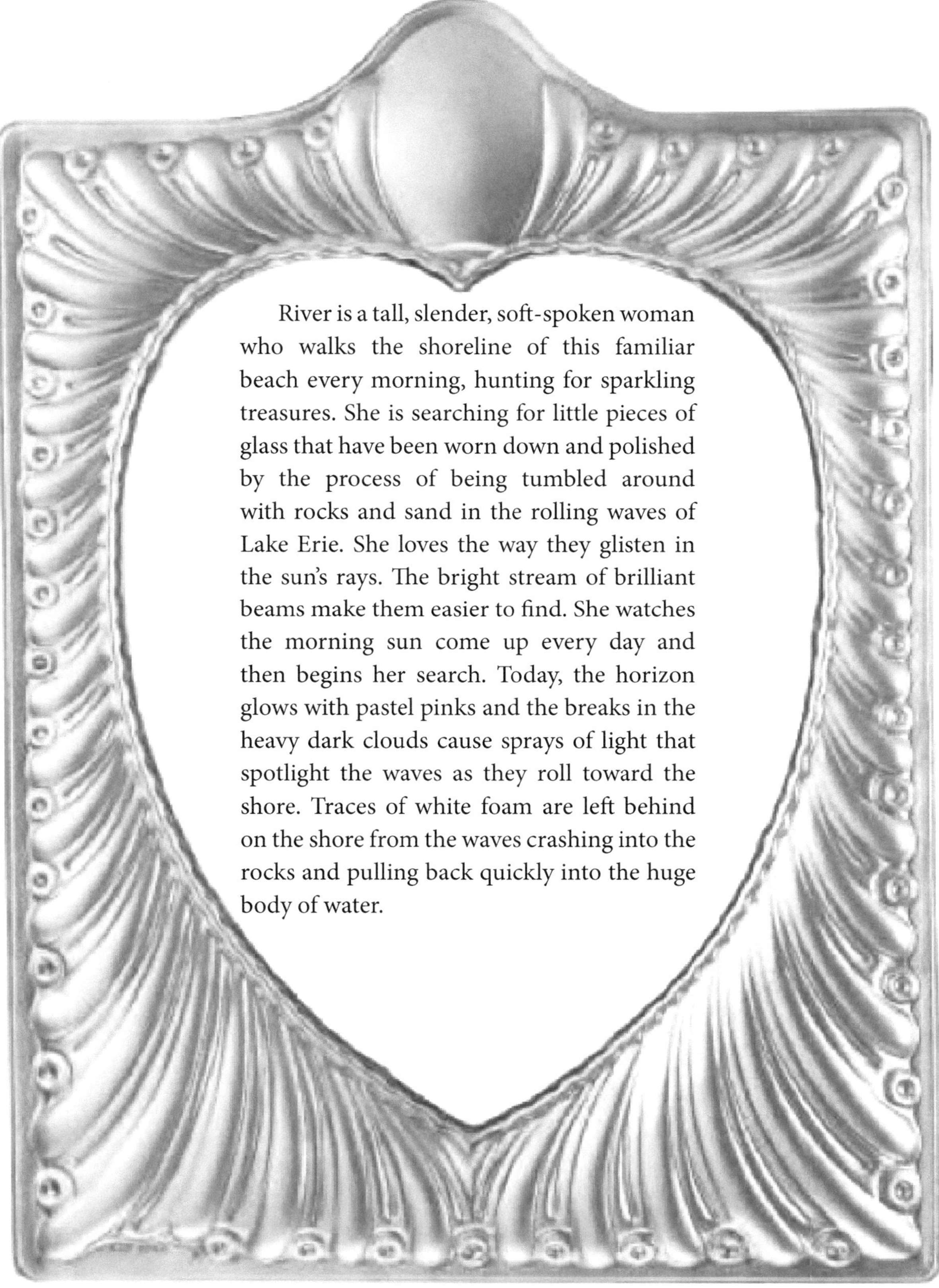

River is a tall, slender, soft-spoken woman who walks the shoreline of this familiar beach every morning, hunting for sparkling treasures. She is searching for little pieces of glass that have been worn down and polished by the process of being tumbled around with rocks and sand in the rolling waves of Lake Erie. She loves the way they glisten in the sun's rays. The bright stream of brilliant beams make them easier to find. She watches the morning sun come up every day and then begins her search. Today, the horizon glows with pastel pinks and the breaks in the heavy dark clouds cause sprays of light that spotlight the waves as they roll toward the shore. Traces of white foam are left behind on the shore from the waves crashing into the rocks and pulling back quickly into the huge body of water.

Hunting for beach glass is not the only reason she comes to Erie's shores. Her heart is full of sorrow and her soul is in anguish. The waves seem to calm her just enough to get her through the day. It is as if every swell is trying to bathe her entire being in peace, but she only allows partial healing, because to let go of the pain entirely, she would have to let go of part of herself.

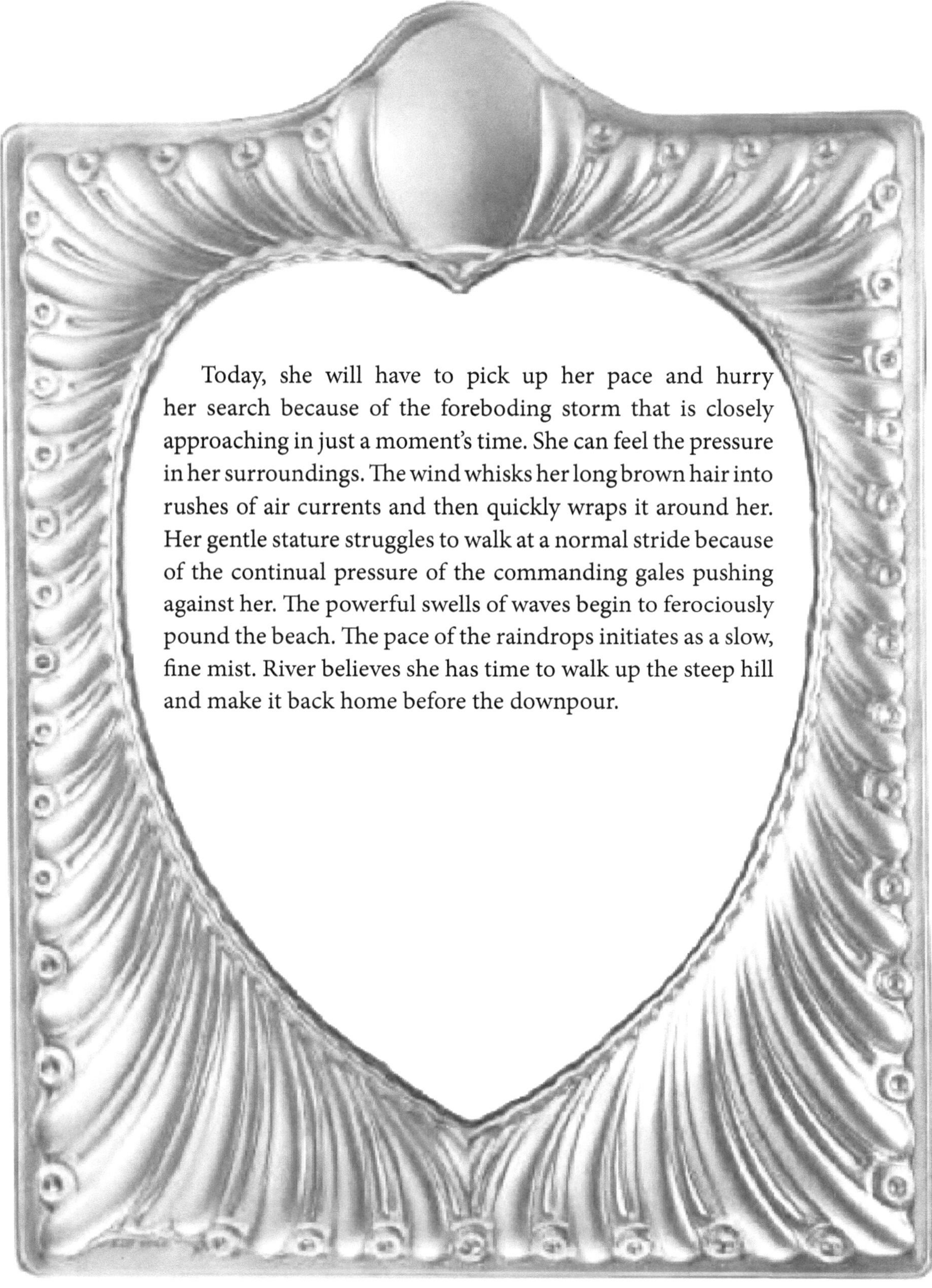

Today, she will have to pick up her pace and hurry her search because of the foreboding storm that is closely approaching in just a moment's time. She can feel the pressure in her surroundings. The wind whisks her long brown hair into rushes of air currents and then quickly wraps it around her. Her gentle stature struggles to walk at a normal stride because of the continual pressure of the commanding gales pushing against her. The powerful swells of waves begin to ferociously pound the beach. The pace of the raindrops initiates as a slow, fine mist. River believes she has time to walk up the steep hill and make it back home before the downpour.

Just as she starts to leave, she hears a soft voice behind her. She turns and sees the silhouette of a small female child in the distance. The child is looking for something in the sand as well, and River thinks that perhaps she, too, is searching for beach glass. She is concerned that this child is too young to be on the beach by herself, and with a storm coming, so she directs her hike toward the child to check on her. The child does not see her coming. She is too busy searching for something among the small rocks.

When River gets close enough she says, "Hello."

The child jumps and says, "You scared me!"

River asks, "What are you looking for?"

The child says, "Something very special to me was lost."

River asks, "Would you like me to help you find it? There is a storm coming, and you should probably take care."

The little girl looks into River's eyes. She pauses, staring at her eyes the same way she had previously been looking through the sand. The little girl says, "You have kind eyes, but why are they sad?"

River replies, "They are sad because my soul is sad." River asks, "Who are you here with? Where are your mother and father?"

The little girl says, "I have no mother. My father told me that she died when I was young, and my father is on his boat."

River introduces herself to the little girl, and the little girl says, "My name is Rain." River starts to ask about Rain's father when the sprinkle turns into a downpour.

Rain tells River, "You had better come with me. You do not have time to get home before the storm gets bad. Come, I have a secret place where we can hide."

"Hide? Why would we hide?" asks River.

Rain hesitates a little and then replies, "From the rain, silly!"

The two of them quickly climb up a cliff and around a bend in the shoreline to a more secluded and quiet place. They safely tuck themselves inside a tree house built under a cluster of trees that Rain calls her rainforest. They sit and talk for hours.

Rain has incredible stories about her animal friends and she tells River about each one, but the most interesting friend is a creature who is like a nanny to her. She has named him Billow because of the big waves he makes as he whirls his lengthy body through the waters of Lake Erie.

Rain explains that Billow is kind of a lake monster who cracks his tail on the cliffs and hides in the waves, and that most humans can't see him. He takes Rain to the shores during storms and takes her back out to the lake as soon as they subside. Rain also tells River that Billow does not trust humans and feels the need to protect her from them, but he is kind to Rain and wants her to be happy.

What she doesn't tell River is that Billow is under a spell to guard Rain from escaping from her father. Billow makes sure she does not leave the shoreline on Rain's father's orders, for he knows that other humans run from the beach when it rains so most likely no one will ever see Rain. Billow also has orders from Rain's father to keep her far away from anyone on the beach or everyone will pay the consequences. What those penalties are no one really knows, because none of Rain's friends, nor Rain, have ever disobeyed him, until now. Rain's father is cruel, and no one knows why he is so harsh with Rain. Billow has learned to see through the spell and now loves Rain and has become more compassionate in dealing with Rain. Rain's love for Billow and his quest for answers is helping to slowly change him.

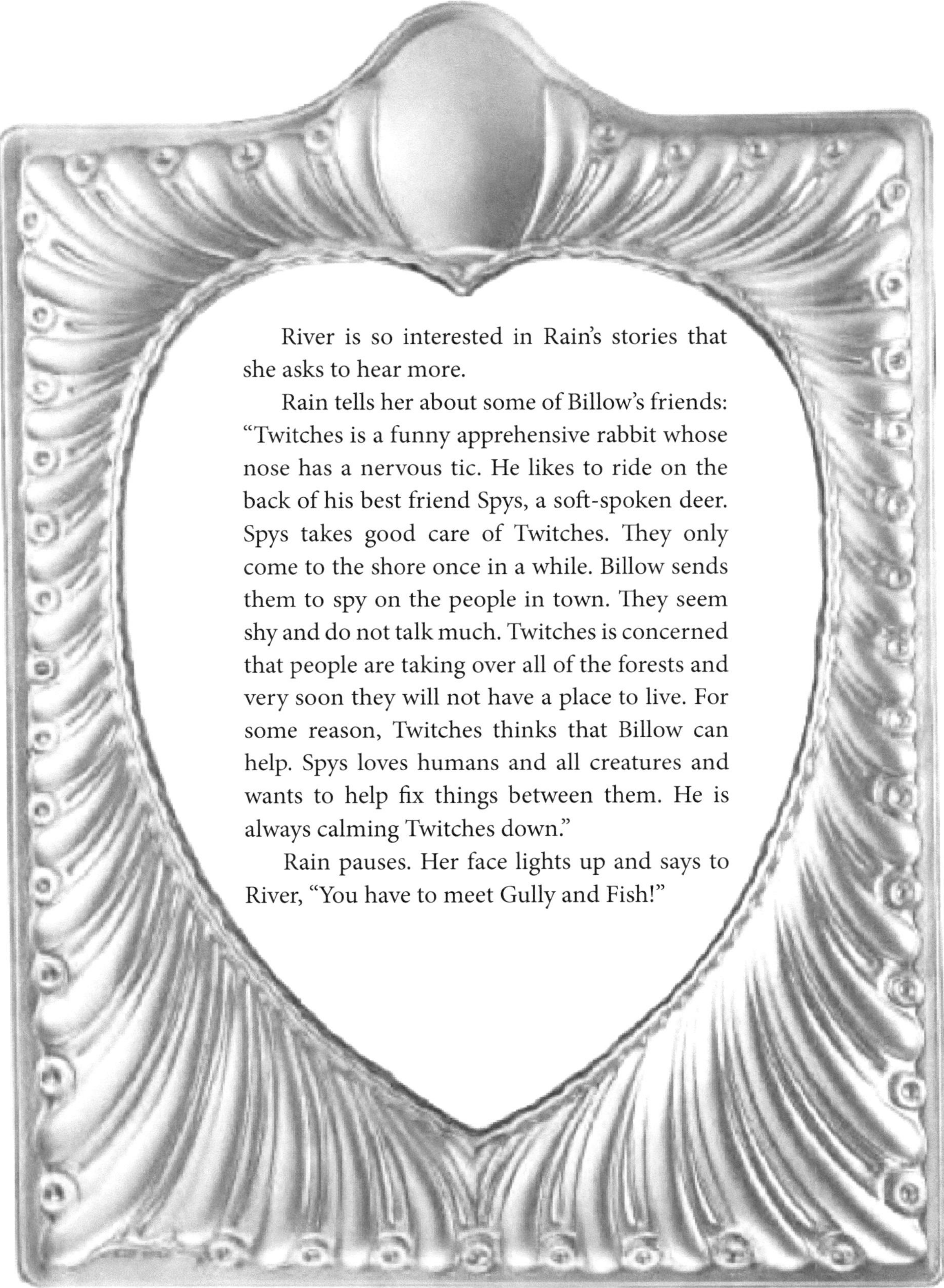

River is so interested in Rain's stories that she asks to hear more.

Rain tells her about some of Billow's friends: "Twitches is a funny apprehensive rabbit whose nose has a nervous tic. He likes to ride on the back of his best friend Spys, a soft-spoken deer. Spys takes good care of Twitches. They only come to the shore once in a while. Billow sends them to spy on the people in town. They seem shy and do not talk much. Twitches is concerned that people are taking over all of the forests and very soon they will not have a place to live. For some reason, Twitches thinks that Billow can help. Spys loves humans and all creatures and wants to help fix things between them. He is always calming Twitches down."

Rain pauses. Her face lights up and says to River, "You have to meet Gully and Fish!"

Rain tells River, "Gully and Fish are two of my favorite friends! They bring me beach glass and tell dumb jokes, which are always followed by a silly laugh."

Rain tells one of their jokes, walks like a seagull, and tries to mimic their laugh, causing River and Rain to giggle out loud.

Rain tells River, "They are under some kind of spell. Most times what they say is such nonsense that I cannot figure it out unless they say it as a riddle or joke. They get so excited and frustrated. One time they tried to tell me something about Billow and it came out all scrambled. They said something like, bilherlowdfatisyrandourgr."

Rain tells River, "They do not try to have conversations anymore. They just tell knock-knock jokes. Sometimes I can get a glimpse into what Gully and Fish are trying to express. They are faithful friends and I do feel sorry for them. I do not remember this, but Billow told me that they used to speak quite elegantly before the spell."

The woman and the child spend the whole morning talking, but it seems like just a few minutes. Rain pauses for a brief moment to take a good look at River. River looks back at Rain.

River breaks the silence by saying, "Your stories are delightful!" Then she asks with a small sparkle of joy in her voice, "Please tell me more!"

Rain is searching her mind to think of things to share with River when, in only a moment, the solitude creeps back in as she remembers years of walking on the shore alone. Even though her short time with River has been wonderful, she knows she has to leave and it will end soon. She remembers that when she walks on the shore she often runs across a group of singing shells. The songs they sing are intriguing so she decides to tell River about them. She tells River that the shells sing to her. She describes them as a choir and tells her that they sing all the time. When no one is around, they sing to the waves and always stay close to the shore. They love to visit with Rain. She tells River that it is odd because their songs bring her comfort but cause her sadness as well. The melodies are always in a minor key and take her back into her childhood, but she cannot remember anything that explains why. As Rain is about to sing her favorite song that she has heard them sing, she and River hear a high-pitched scream.

River starts to run out of the tree house to see what is wrong when Rain says, "Don't worry. That's just Shakes."

Rain gets up and opens the door for Shakes so he can come in out of the rain. Shakes is a snake that is very timid and is afraid of everything. Because he seems to always be trembling in fear, Rain named him Shakes.

"More friends?" asks River

Rain smiles at River and replies, "Yes! I have a few more to tell you about. River, meet Shakes!"

He is upset that River is there, and Rain has to calm him down. He is always warning Rain about other humans and is very afraid of Rain's father. Rain shares with River how Shakes screams like a girl when it thunders. This makes Rain laugh. She pokes fun at him, saying, "Is the big bad snakey-wakey afraid of the big bad thunder-wunder?"

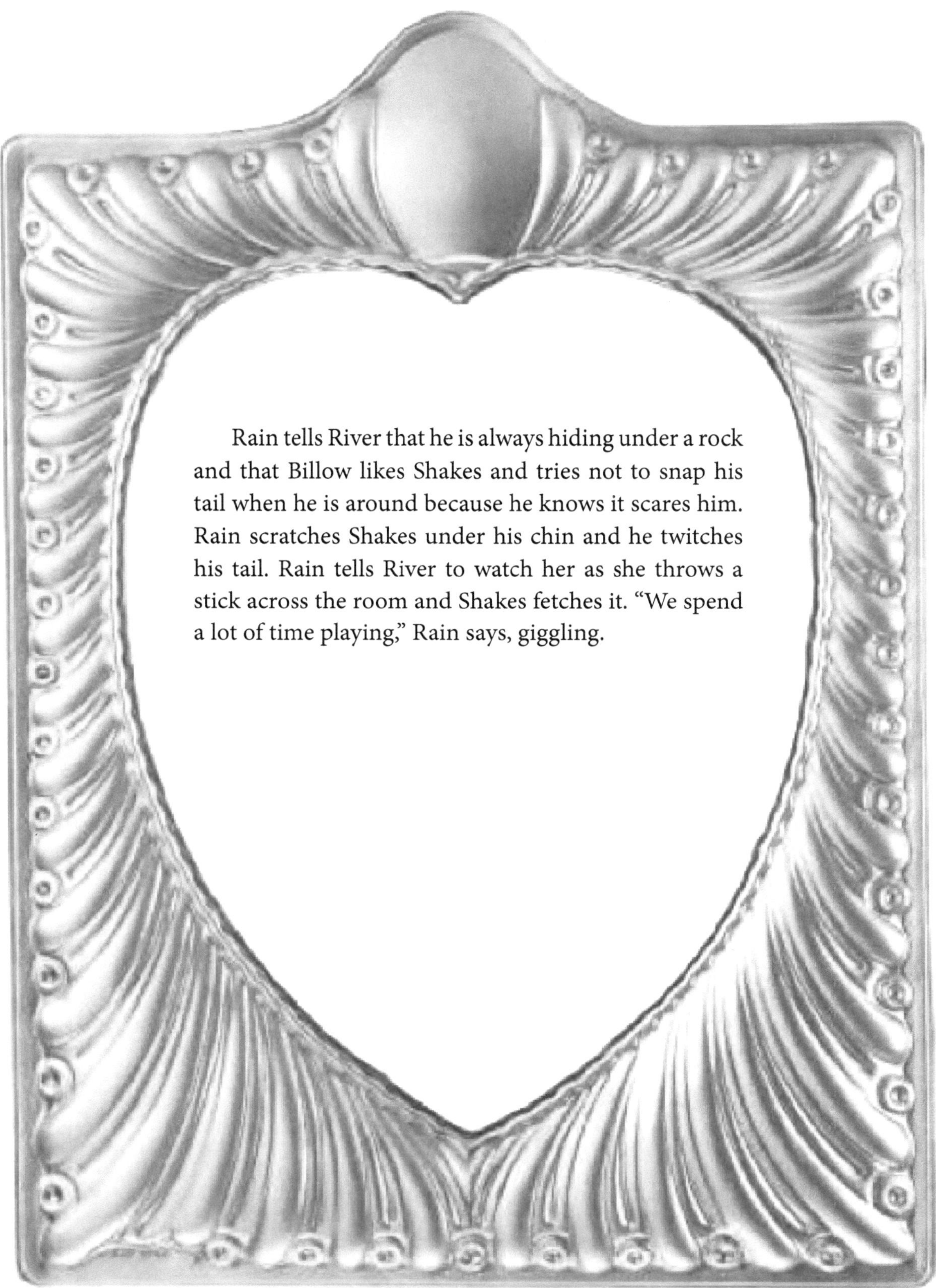

Rain tells River that he is always hiding under a rock and that Billow likes Shakes and tries not to snap his tail when he is around because he knows it scares him. Rain scratches Shakes under his chin and he twitches his tail. Rain tells River to watch her as she throws a stick across the room and Shakes fetches it. "We spend a lot of time playing," Rain says, giggling.

Just then, Rain, River, and Shakes hear a loud cracking sound. Rain jumps up suddenly and says, "Oh, no. The rain has stopped."

Shakes yells, "That is Billow. You've got to go! Hurry, Rain. You do not want to get your dad angry. You know how he is!"

River yells, "Wait!" as her two new friends run out the door in a great hurry. "I want to see you again, Rain. Please, may I see you again?"

River starts to come out of the tree house when Shakes yells, "No! Billow will see you, and we will all be in trouble!"

Rain yells back to Shakes, "Tell River I can meet her at the next storm. Come and wait at my rainforest and I will come."

Shakes tells Rain, "Are you crazy? What if your dad finds out?"

"He won't," says Rain. "I will keep her hidden."

River overhears them and ducks back in the tree house. She has almost forgotten her sadness for a few brief hours, and she loves to hear of this little girl's tales. It makes her feel alive again.

Many days pass, and because the skies have been clear, River does not see Rain. River always visits the tree house just in case.

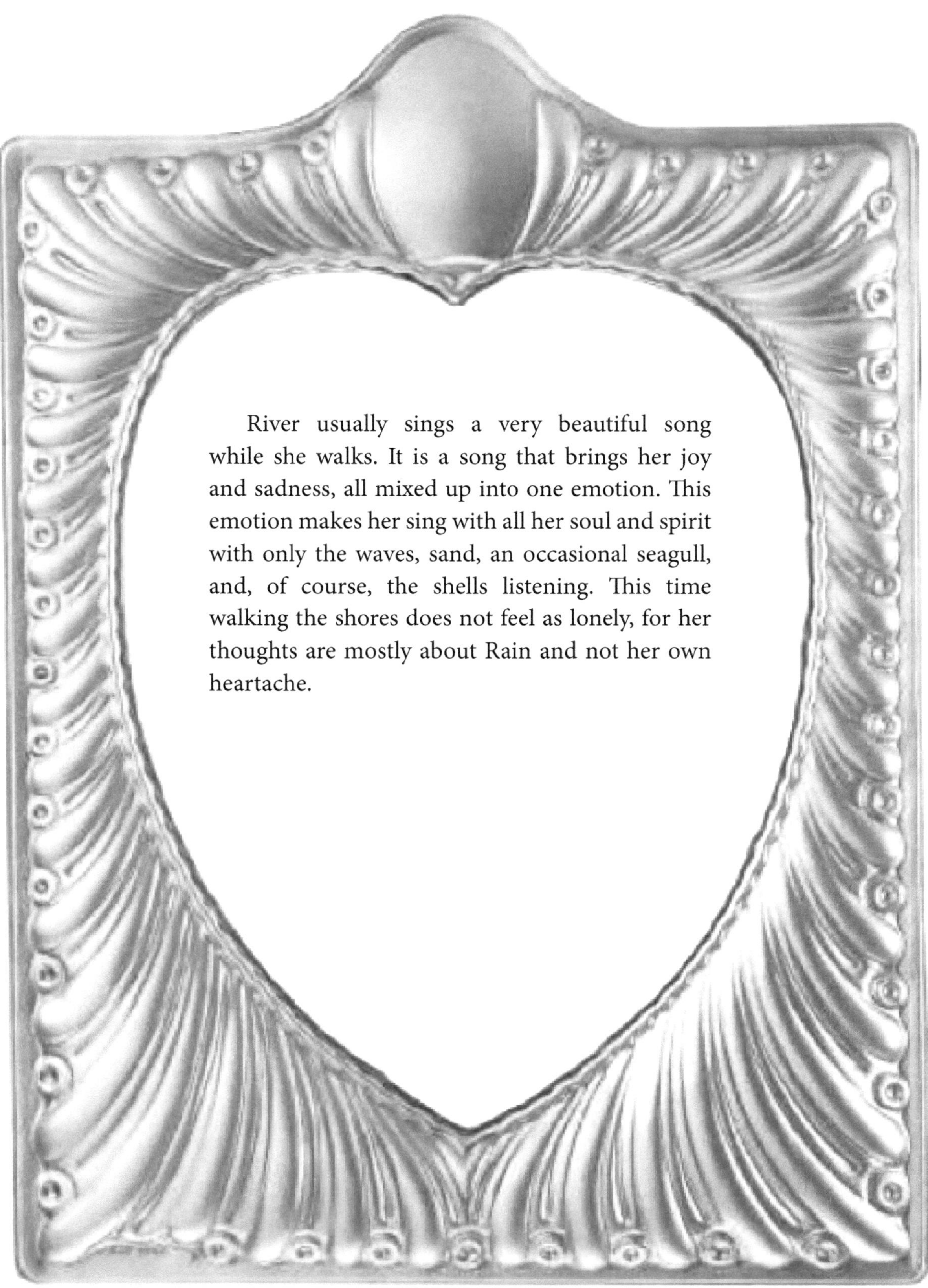

River usually sings a very beautiful song while she walks. It is a song that brings her joy and sadness, all mixed up into one emotion. This emotion makes her sing with all her soul and spirit with only the waves, sand, an occasional seagull, and, of course, the shells listening. This time walking the shores does not feel as lonely, for her thoughts are mostly about Rain and not her own heartache.

One morning while River is hunting the shore for treasures, she finds something quite beautiful. It is an old crystal-heart bottle stopper, but the odd part about it is that it looks carefully placed in the center of a circle made of seven beautiful pieces of beach glass. She picks it up and takes it home. She loves it so much that she drills a hole through it and makes it into a necklace that she wants to wear every day. Somehow, it makes her feel closer to Rain.

In just one meeting, this little girl stole her heart. River feels maybe she could help her since Rain has no mother. She thinks that maybe she could be there for Rain when she needs a woman's influence, and maybe it could somehow make her feel better about her own loss.

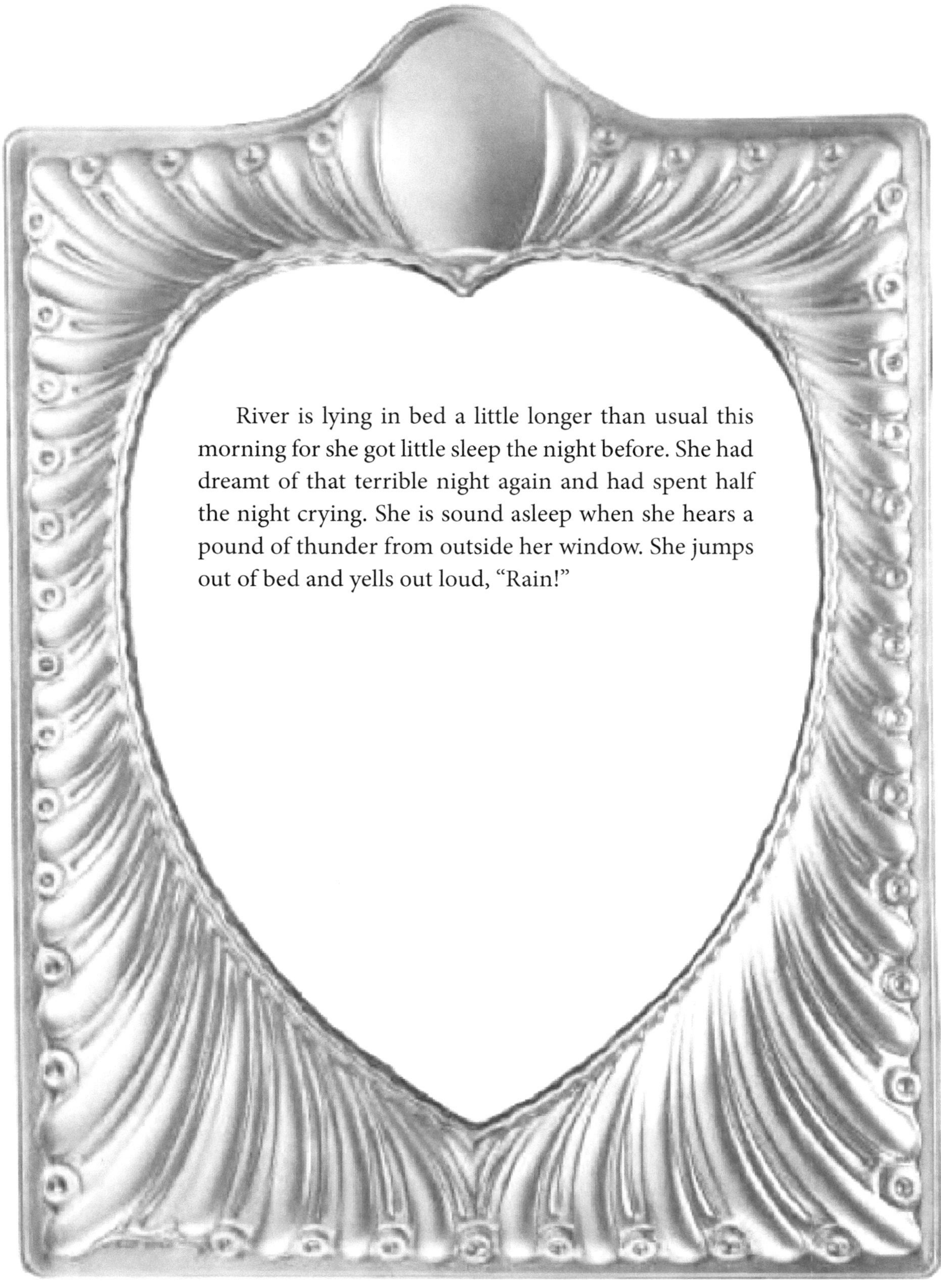

River is lying in bed a little longer than usual this morning for she got little sleep the night before. She had dreamt of that terrible night again and had spent half the night crying. She is sound asleep when she hears a pound of thunder from outside her window. She jumps out of bed and yells out loud, "Rain!"

Back at the lake, Rain is just arriving on Billow's back when Spys comes up to the lake to meet them. He has Twitches on his back. Many of Rain's friends have gathered to welcome Rain as well.

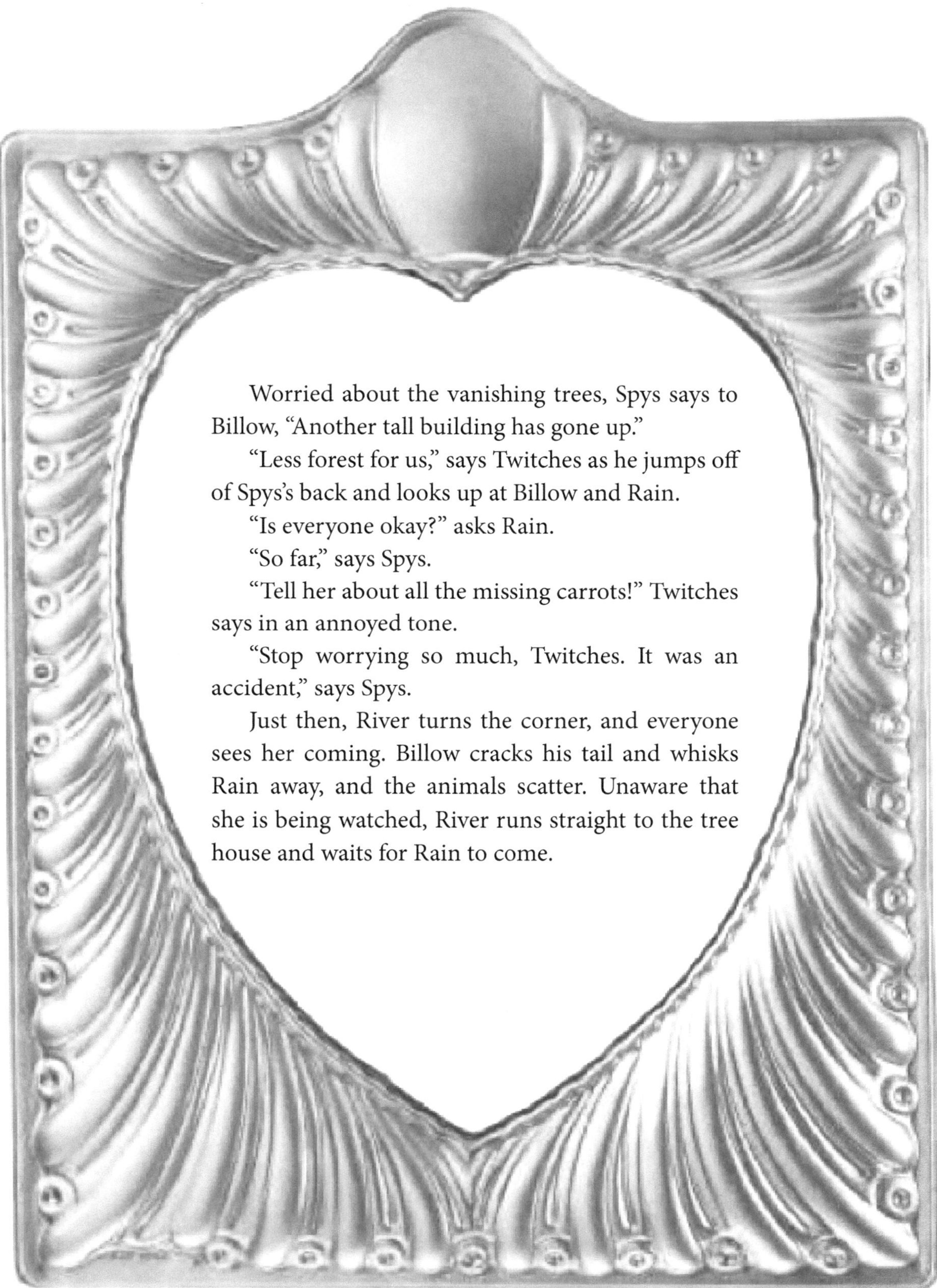

Worried about the vanishing trees, Spys says to Billow, "Another tall building has gone up."

"Less forest for us," says Twitches as he jumps off of Spys's back and looks up at Billow and Rain.

"Is everyone okay?" asks Rain.

"So far," says Spys.

"Tell her about all the missing carrots!" Twitches says in an annoyed tone.

"Stop worrying so much, Twitches. It was an accident," says Spys.

Just then, River turns the corner, and everyone sees her coming. Billow cracks his tail and whisks Rain away, and the animals scatter. Unaware that she is being watched, River runs straight to the tree house and waits for Rain to come.

It takes some time for Rain to convince Billow to let her go. Shakes tells Billow about River and that she seems to be nice and could be good company for Rain. Rain looks lovingly into Billow's eyes and Billow weakens. Billow reluctantly lets her go, but he calls to one of Rain's friends, a raccoon named Chewy, to go with her to keep an eye on things. Chewy is always munching on something. He even eats leftover picnic lunches that people have left behind! He is either going through the garbage or fishing every time Rain runs into him. He is always talking with his mouth at least half full.

As Rain and Chewy arrive at the tree house, Chewy sees some food wrappers that have blown against the tree. He tells Rain to go on in and that he will join her in a second because he wants to investigate the litter.

River, filled with relief when she sees Rain, exclaims, "You came! I am so glad. I have missed you."

Rain says, "I always come when it storms. I am always so glad to get off my father's boat."

River starts to ask about Rain's father when Rain interrupts and asks her, "Why are you so sad?"

"Oh," says River, "It is a long story. Maybe sometime I will tell you."

Rain asks, "Why not now?"

River has tears coming down her cheeks when she replies, "Oh, it has been a bad night for me. I dreamt about that night."

Rain asks lovingly, "What night?"

River starts to really cry and says, "The night he took…"

River hesitates, so Rain asks, "Who took what?"

Just then, the building intensity of pounding waves strikes a cliff and causes River and Rain to pause, listen, and take in the sounds of the powerful storm around them. Abruptly, Chewy leaps through the door and startles them.

Rain jumps back and in a soft, frightened voice shouts, "Chewy! You frightened us!" Chewy is excited, so he ignores her comment and asks Rain to read to him the ingredients off of some wrappers he has gathered up. Rain shakes her head, smiles, and says to River, "And this is Chewy."

Rain starts to read to Chewy. As she reads it, he imagines what the food might taste like. While Rain reads the ingredients, Chewy licks his lips and this makes River laugh. Chewy quietly says to himself, "Yummy! Delightful! Wonderful!" Then he pardons himself.

Chewy gives her another piece of paper that he has found and as Rain begins to read what is written on the paper, tears start to form in her eyes. Then she cries out, "She never got it. My mother really is dead." She runs out of the tree house in tears, and River starts to follow her.

Chewy says, "Oh, now I have gone and done it. That must have been the letter that Rain wrote to her mother." Chewy blocks River from going out. He says to her, "Just give her a minute. She'll come back."

"Can you tell me what is wrong?" asks River.

Chewy answers, "Oh, no, I cannot. I will get an evil spell put on me, too."

"Please tell me," begs River. She then pulls out the lunch she had packed for herself and Rain in hopes of using it to bribe Chewy into telling her what she so desperately needs to know. Chewy cannot help himself. He just has to have the sandwich that River is waving in front of his nose.

"Mmm, my favorite, salami!" he says. "Okay, it was the letter that she wrote to her mother. Rain was crying because she knows now that her mother never got her letter. She wrote a note to her mother and put it in a bottle."

River interrupts, "I thought her mother was dead."

"Well, we are not sure," Chewy says in an unconvincing way. "We don't know, but we think her father lied. At least that is what the big, sly old clam, Foxy, told us. She is crafty and smart as a fox. Nobody can outfox her."

"What clam? What does she know?" asks River.

"Could I have another sandwich?" asks Chewy.

"Okay, okay, take Rain's then," River says in a frustrated tone.

"The clam says she knows the whole story but she never told Rain because she was afraid she would go looking for her mother and her father would kill all Rain's friends and her mother. She says she was there that night. She was quite small then. She used to fit in Rain's hand and now she is big enough that Rain sometimes hides inside her when she's crying and needs to be alone."

"How did Rain find out then?" asks River.

"Anything more in that bag?" Chewy asks, smacking his lips.

"Here are some grapes," River says quickly.

Chewy answers, "Well, Fish and Gully know the whole story. They saw it too and they started to tell Rain. Her father put a spell on them. Now, no one will speak the whole truth."

River asks, "Who is her father?"

"I can't tell you!" yells Chewy.

"Where is he?" exclaims River.

"I do not know," says Chewy.

"What else do you know?" asks River, shaking Chewy.

"What else do you got to eat?" he replies.

While Chewy is earning his lunch, Rain is crying on the beach. As she sits with her head tucked in her arms, the shell choir comes out and sings to her to calm her like they always do. This time, they sing River's song. Again, Rain thinks it sounds familiar, and it makes her feel happy and sad all at the same time, just like River. Suddenly, Gully and Fish come up to Rain and try to tell her a joke.

"Not now!" says Rain sadly. "I am crying."

Gully and Fish persist.

Gully says, "Knock knock."

Fish says, "Who's there?"

Gully replies, "Bottle stopper."

Fish asks, "Bottle stopper who?"

Gully says, "Bottle stopper mom." They both laugh, ha ha ha ha. "Stop it! You are not making sense. Leave me alone!" Rain shouts. They keep saying the same joke over and over, so Rain runs off.

Back at the tree house, River continues asking Chewy more questions. "What is her father's name?" she asks.

"I cannot tell you. We will all be in great danger!" shrieks Chewy.

"Tell me," shouts River even louder, grabbing Chewy.

"Okay, okay," says Chewy. "We just call him the Traveler."

River yells, "The Traveler from Canada?"

"Yes," says Chewy. "Now give me another snack."

"Wait!" says River. "The clam, the one she sleeps in, does it have Sandy written on it?"

"Yeah, why?" asks Chewy as he is stuffing himself.

River whispers to herself, "It can't be."

River can hear the crack of Billow's tail and she knows that sound means Rain will be leaving in minutes. She feels anxiousness creep into her body with lightning speed. She rushes to the door but pauses there.

Thoughts are rushing through her mind. She shouts, "Wait! She would be almost twelve years old." River yells in the direction of Chewy, "Listen, tell me now! You can have anything I have! I will bring you food every day! Just please tell me. Is her mother alive?"

"Yes," says Chewy. "Yes, and she lives in town."

With that, River throws her food down and runs to the beach.

River sees Rain on Billow's back and yells to her, "Rain, Rain!" as she runs to the shore.

Rain leaves with Billow.

Billow sees River running and yelling at Rain to stop, but he ducks under the water with Rain. River stands on the shore, longing to talk to Rain.

Suddenly she sees Billow's tail, and she sees Rain. She
says to herself, "They are coming back!" River waits until
Rain comes ashore.
Rain says softly, "Billow saw me crying and said I
must talk to you. He said it is time. What did he mean?"
"I think I know. Sit down, Rain," River says gently.

Billow dives under the water and cracks his tail softly this time, as if he is saying to Rain, I know you both need some time, but I am nearby if you need me.

River knows it is time to tell Rain about her pain and to reveal to her what has caused her sorrow. She looks lovingly at Rain, searching her face for an indication of what she may be thinking, but sees only signs of her plight on her face. River softly says to Rain, "I know about you, but let me tell you a little about me."

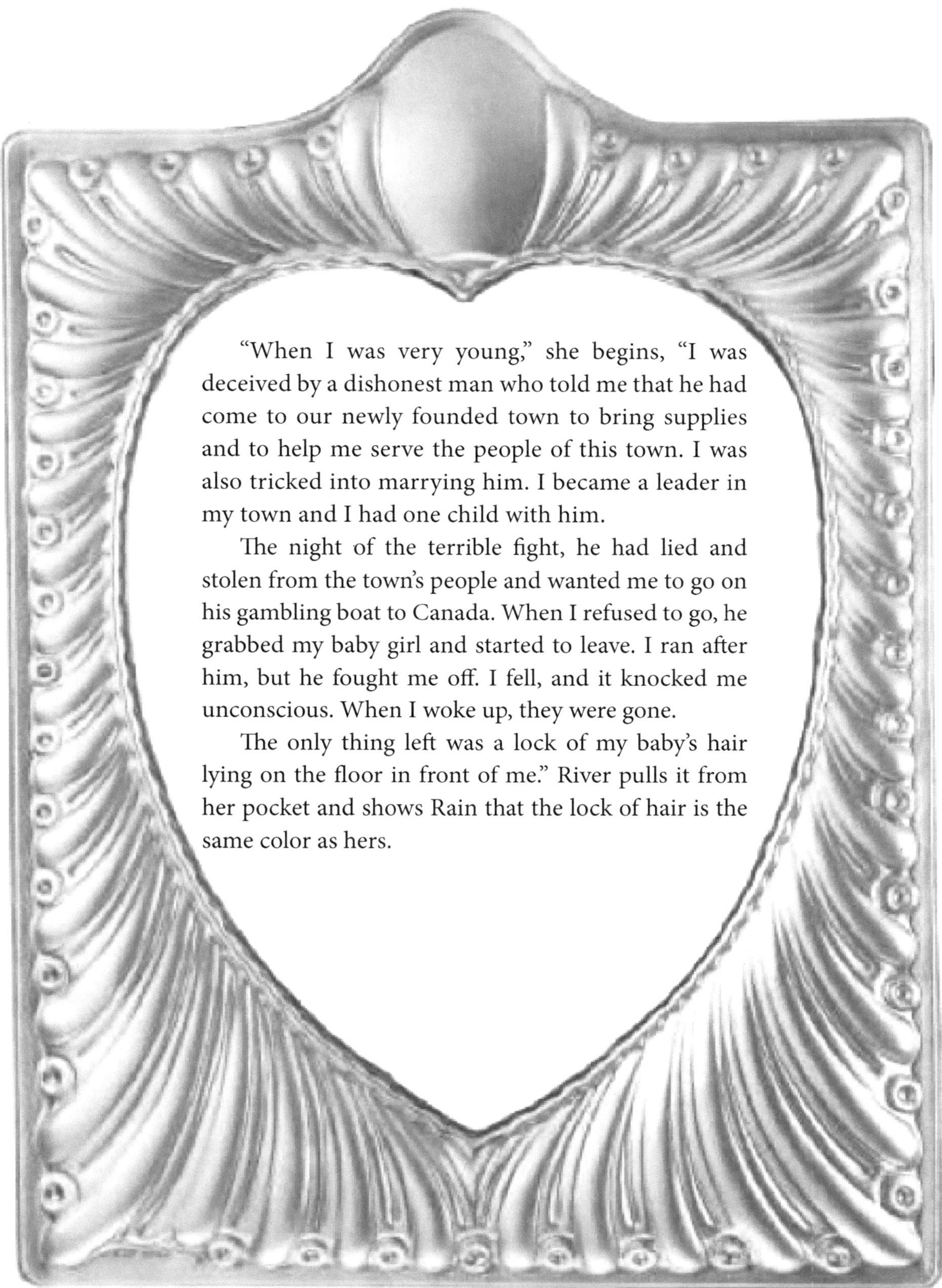

"When I was very young," she begins, "I was deceived by a dishonest man who told me that he had come to our newly founded town to bring supplies and to help me serve the people of this town. I was also tricked into marrying him. I became a leader in my town and I had one child with him.

The night of the terrible fight, he had lied and stolen from the town's people and wanted me to go on his gambling boat to Canada. When I refused to go, he grabbed my baby girl and started to leave. I ran after him, but he fought me off. I fell, and it knocked me unconscious. When I woke up, they were gone.

The only thing left was a lock of my baby's hair lying on the floor in front of me." River pulls it from her pocket and shows Rain that the lock of hair is the same color as hers.

"No!" says Rain. "My mom is dead. She never got my letter. Foxy told me that she sprinkled all of the magic that was left in her pearl on the bottle with the letter, and that it would reach my mother if she was still alive. It didn't!"

"Wait," says River. "Does your clam have 'Sandy' written on her? I gave a small clam to my daughter when she was very young. It had Sandy written on it. That was my mother's name."

"Yes," says Rain. "But Chewy probably told you that. He will tell you anything for a cookie."

"Wait!" says River. "Please let me finish. I ran to try to catch my husband's boat. When I had reached the lake's shore, I could see his boat in the distance, but it was too far off to catch up to. I fell to the ground and cried until the sun had gone."

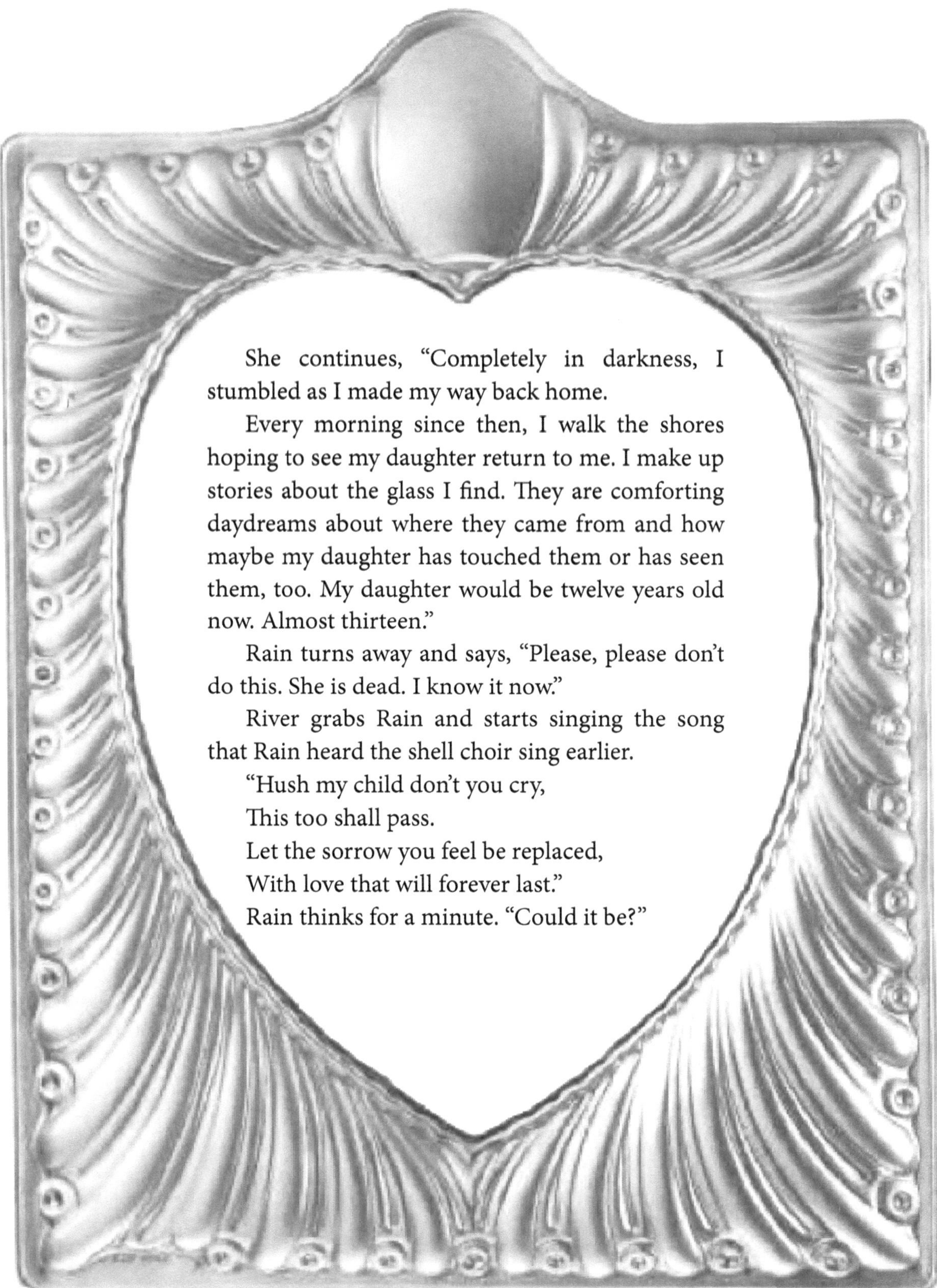

She continues, "Completely in darkness, I stumbled as I made my way back home.

Every morning since then, I walk the shores hoping to see my daughter return to me. I make up stories about the glass I find. They are comforting daydreams about where they came from and how maybe my daughter has touched them or has seen them, too. My daughter would be twelve years old now. Almost thirteen."

Rain turns away and says, "Please, please don't do this. She is dead. I know it now."

River grabs Rain and starts singing the song that Rain heard the shell choir sing earlier.

"Hush my child don't you cry,
This too shall pass.
Let the sorrow you feel be replaced,
With love that will forever last."
Rain thinks for a minute. "Could it be?"

Rain asks herself, "Is she alive?" She breaks away and thinks, "How can it be?" She starts to run back to Billow when Shakes gathers all of his strength and yells to Billow, "Tell her, Billow! Tell us all the truth!"

Billow yells, "Stop!" and jumps up out of the water, dives under, and cracks his tail on the way down. He resurfaces and pauses for a brief moment.

Billow looks deep into Rain's eyes and tells her what he knows. He tells her about the curse her father put on Gully and Fish because they were about to tell her that her mother was alive.

Surprised, Rain looks at River, then Billow, and then asks, "What are you saying?"

Billow replies, "It is possible!"

Gully and Fish get everyone's attention by starting to tell their knock-knock joke again.

Then Rain turns to River and looks into River's eyes with hope swelling in her heart.

The shells start singing River's song, which causes tears to form in Rain's searching eyes.

Rain is running memories through her mind, looking for answers. River finds the longing unbearable, for she has ached to embrace her child again for many years. Just as River starts to run to Rain, Rain yells, "Stop!"

River stops and drops to sit on a large piece of driftwood. Her heart is beating fast and she needs to rest to try to slow it a bit. Rain runs to River to see if she is okay. When she looks down at River she notices the crystal-heart bottle stopper hanging on a chain around River's neck. Rain yells, "Where did you get that?"

River stands and says, "I found it on the beach."

Gully and Fish are jumping in excitement. The shell choir is still singing River's song and Chewy and Shakes are cuddled together watching this intense scene.

Rain says in a whisper, "You are my mother. You did find it! The letter I wrote my mother was in a bottle sealed with that crystal-heart bottle stopper!" She embraces River as she cries out, "You are my mother!"

Mother and daughter are truly united, but what will happen now? Will Rain be able to stay with her mother? What will happen if she does not return with Billow when the storm passes? Will her father keep his promise and hurt Rain's friends and her mother? What can they do to protect themselves? The two characters have to work through much heartache before they are through this dilemma and are safe from Rain's father. See if you can guess what will happen before the next book is published.

Milton Keynes UK
Ingram Content Group UK Ltd.
UKHW050354050224
437138UK00004B/48